C000104492

LOST BUILDINGS OF
NOTTINGHAM

DOUGLAS WHITWORTH

To Margaret with my love

The Old Moot Hall, Wheeler Gate, in 1925 – a mock-Tudor replacement for the original seventeenth-century building (see pages 8 and 9).

Title page photograph: Radford Folly in 1923. The last remains of Radford Grove – the nearest approach to London's Vauxhall Gardens which Nottingham possessed. The pleasure gardens laid out in 1780 by William Elliott survived for almost a century.

First published 2010
Reprinted 2012

The History Press
The Mill, Brimscombe Port
Stroud, Gloucestershire, GL5 2QG
www.thehistorypress.co.uk

British Library Cataloguing in Publication Data.
A catalogue record for this book is available from the British Library.

ISBN 978 0 7524 5487 0

Typesetting and origination by The History Press
Printed in Great Britain

CONTENTS

Drury Hill in 1922. This is one of the oldest streets in Nottingham and certainly the most photogenic. The shop on the right with a hanging sign is Higham's shoe business, established in 1848. The street was demolished in 1968 to the dismay of most Nottingham people.

INTRODUCTION

Buildings in Nottingham of great or little value have been lost in the last century for many reasons. In some cases the destruction has been deliberate – by politicians who had either an axe to grind or who decided that the architecture around them was out-of-date and needed to be replaced. Some property developers see buildings as commodities which can be purchased and destroyed without consideration of their architectural value. Other causes of destruction of buildings include acts of war, which in the case of this city was mainly during the Blitz of 8/9 May 1941. Other losses in Nottingham have been the result of fashion – for example the change from cinema-going to television viewing and the consequent loss of most of the suburban cinemas, a number of them wonderful examples of Art Deco architecture. The first loss of an important building in the twentieth century was the destruction of the Albert Hall in 1906. The Wesleyan Chapel, designed by Watson Fothergill, was destroyed in one of the most spectacular fires seen in the city and the roofless shell was subsequently demolished. Construction began immediately on a new Albert Hall in Italianate style, mainly funded by Jesse Boot.

The city centre has seen the greatest wanton destruction of important buildings. In the 1920s the planned widening of Friar Lane threatened Dorothy Vernon's house with demolition. This Tudor building was one of the city's last links with the medieval era, built as it was on the foundations of a Carmelite Friary which dated back to the thirteenth century. Despite determined efforts by conservationists, this historic house was pulled down in 1927.

The demolition of the old Exchange to be replaced in 1929 by the landmark Council House was no great loss. The building had little character and sheltered the unsavoury Shambles and a number of old public houses. In 1932 an apparent bargain of the century was bought at auction, when St Heliers, the huge mansion previously owned by Jesse Boot, came up for sale. With little interest in the property, the house was sold for £7 to a builder whose aim was to convert the building into flats. In the event the house was pulled down to be replaced by Territorial Army officers' quarters.

The 1920s and '30s were the decades when the city authorities began clearing the Broad and Narrow Marshes of slum properties, including the notorious back-to-back houses which blighted the image of Nottingham. The City Council had been stung into action by the judgement of the Minister of Health when he refused the council's application to extend the city's boundaries to encompass the surrounding suburbs. Most of the properties were among the worst in Britain but several Tudor dwellings were pulled down in the wholesale clearance of the areas. The council took advantage of the opportunity offered by the demolition in staging a civil defence exercise there – a chilling foretaste of things to come.

The wartime Blitz, while not as devastating as in other British cities, destroyed numerous buildings and caused hundreds of casualties. Among the most important losses in the city were the Old Moot Hall in Wheeler Gate, part of the University College, St John's and St Christopher's Churches and the Register Office.

After the war, the City Council continued the razing of Broad Marsh and also began the demolition of the district east of the castle before the construction of the first stage of a planned inner ring road. While many of the buildings cleared in this area were of little value, two of the properties demolished were of great importance. The St Nicholas Rectory, designed by Watson Fothergill, was a notable casualty, but the demolition of the Collin's Almshouses in Friar Lane was controversial and unnecessary. These almshouses, while needing only internal improvements, were externally among the most attractive in the country. The building of Maid Marian Way only required the demolition of the outbuildings of the almshouses, and although determined efforts were made to save the building, it was reduced to rubble in 1956.

The 1960s was the decade when the City Council allowed the worst decimation of inner city Nottingham to occur. When in 1964 the Victoria railway station was threatened with closure under the Beeching axe, the land was sold for development as a shopping centre. The project was to include a sports centre, hotel, cinema and a concert hall, though none of these were built. The loss of the splendid Victoria station with its direct line to London has been bemoaned ever since.

Equally contentious was the building of the shopping centre to the south of the city centre on the cleared land of Broad Marsh. The area had been undeveloped since before the war but in 1968 Drury Hill – the ancient and picturesque route from Middle Pavement to the south – was threatened with demolition. Protestations by local civic groups were to no avail, nor was the advice to incorporate the street into the centre, to rival the reconstructed shopping street in the Castle Museum in York.

Also threatened with destruction was the fifteenth-century Severn's building on Middle Pavement, but this was saved and dismantled before being re-erected on Castle Road. The adjoining Georgian house was not so fortunate and was demolished.

The Broad Marsh Centre has never been as successful as the Victoria Centre and is criticised for its brutal architecture. Now the centre's commercial luck has run out; there are plans for its complete demolition and rebuilding.

The late 1960s saw what many citizens regard as the worst act of vandalism when the Black Boy Hotel was allowed to be demolished. When the lease on the property expired in 1961, Littlewoods bought the site from Brunts Charity and despite protests from civic bodies, the wonderful and fanciful Watson Fothergill building was pulled down in 1970 to be replaced by a faceless department store.

The Old Market Square was also disfigured in the 1960s by a functional office block replacing the traditional 1920s Lloyds Bank building. The thirteen-storey block, although set back from Beastmarket Hill, violates the building heights of the square.

The historic Lace Market was then becoming run down with the closure of many lace warehouses. Although some of the Victorian buildings became multi-tenanted, many of the handsome warehouses were pulled down leaving unsightly gaps in the streets. However, before irreparable damage was done, the City Council, in conjunction with the Lace Market Development Company, began the restoration of the area. Many of the remaining lace warehouses have now been converted into flats and smart new office and apartment blocks have been built on the vacant land. An area which at one time seemed destined to be beyond redemption has now seen a renaissance.

Two inner city areas which were to see an almost complete rebuilding in the 1970s were St Ann's and the Meadows. Both districts were mainly Victorian, the dwellings of which were by then substandard and judged to be beyond repair. St Ann's was almost entirely cleared in that decade, including most of the churches and public houses. The rebuilt houses and flats sadly have less character than the old terraces and the new precincts are soulless and uninspiring.

The Meadows suffered a similar fate to St Ann's, being almost completely obliterated apart from some of the better-built houses towards the River Trent. Arkwright Street, which was the main artery to Trent Bridge, was truncated with the loss of dozens of small shops which had served almost all the needs of the local community. After less than forty years there are now plans to redesign the precincts and walkways which were a blight on the area.

A long-awaited city project came to fruition in the late 1970s with the building of a modern concert hall. This had been on the drawing board since the end of the Second World War and was being built on the site of the Empire Theatre – the Victorian variety theatre had closed in 1958, a victim of falling attendances. The County Hotel adjoining the Theatre Royal was also demolished, robbing Nottingham of its closest approach to a Regency terrace.

After the excessive clearances of the 1960s and '70s the following decades saw a welcome respite from unthinking destruction. One of the regrettable exceptions was the closure of the Flying Horse Hotel, followed by the demolition of the interior, leaving only the mock-Tudor frontage. The building has now been opened as a shopping mall with the uninspiring name – F.H. Mall.

The Italianate Old Market Square which existed for over seventy years, has been completely redesigned and although not a structure, deserves mention as a feature which complemented the classical Council House.

The photographs in this book show many fine buildings of the city, most of which have been lost in the lifetime of the majority of the citizens of Nottingham. Also included are some of the substandard houses which marred Nottingham's reputation in the early part of the twentieth century. It is to be hoped that the city authorities will learn from past mistakes and in future preserve the best of Nottingham's rich heritage.

Long Row East in 1936, with pedestrians apparently unconcerned by the traffic swirling around them. The wonderful Black Boy Hotel in the background was demolished in 1970 in an unbelievable act of vandalism.

The Old Moot Hall at the corner of Wheeler Gate and Friar Lane, 1895. The building dated from the seventeenth century when it was known as the Feathers Inn. In 1689 the local gentry met here when it was the temporary residence of Lord Delamere, to decide whether they would remain loyal to James II or transfer their allegiance to William of Orange and his wife Mary, daughter of the king. Their decision to support William and Mary met with the full approval of the town's citizens. In 1900 the Old Moot Hall was unaccountably demolished and replaced with a mock-Tudor building (see page 2).

❧ 1 ❧

THE CITY CENTRE

The ruins of the Old Moot Hall after the Blitz of 8/9 May 1941. The mock-Tudor building was almost entirely destroyed, but fortunately, there were no casualties. This was the only serious air raid on Nottingham during the Second World War, with 159 people killed and many more injured. Besides the loss of this building there were several other major casualties and hundreds of houses were destroyed or rendered unfit for habitation. The worst incident was at the Co-operative Bakery on Meadow Lane where forty-nine employees and members of the Home Guard were killed.

Dorothy Vernon's house, Friar Lane, in 1921, was one of the oldest houses in the city, with a romantic history. The Carmelite or White Friars established their friary here in 1271 and gradually extended their building along Friar Row, the present Beastmarket Hill to St James's Street. After the friary was dissolved in 1539, a house was built on the site to which John Musters and Dorothy Vernon of Haddon Hall eloped in 1572. The house remained relatively undisturbed until the 1920s when the City Council planned to widen Friar Lane, with the consequent loss of this building. Although great efforts were made to save it, the old house was pulled down in 1927.

The Oriental Café, Wheeler Gate, 1944. Dating from the seventeenth century, this was then owned by Lord Mansfield. When occupied by Armitage Brothers as a café in the early part of the twentieth century, the ground floor was decorated in Japanese style, with alcoves along one wall – a prominent feature was a huge coffee-grinding machine. When in 1960 it was proposed to demolish the building, the magnificent Jacobean plaster ceiling of the first floor was fortunately saved. Only one specialist firm was prepared to carry out the removal at an extremely high price and the City Council undertook the task themselves. Originally intended for Newdigate House, the plasterwork was taken to Holme Pierrepont Hall where it remained in sections until 1998 when it was installed in a house in Ladbroke Square in London.

Four old-established businesses in Lister Gate in 1950. Boots Cash Chemists had branches in most high streets. Weavers, having been founded in 1844, was bought in 1897 by George Trease and continues to be run by the same family. Besides having a retail shop, there was also an entrance to a public bar which connected to a smoke room in Castle Gate. Dewhursts the butchers and Lennon Brothers, tobacconists, both had several branches in the city. These Victorian buildings were demolished in 1960 before this corner was redeveloped.

Queen Elizabeth II walking along the Processional Way on her visit to the city in 1955, the first time since her accession to the throne. The redesigned Old Market Square of 1929 was well-suited to formal occasions such as these. The buildings on Beastmarket Hill in the background were all to be replaced within twenty years. As the name implies this was the site of the cattle market until it was moved to Burton Street in 1855.

Two of the Victorian buildings on Beastmarket Hill in 1952. King's Restaurant, situated in the basement, was a well-known rendezvous for businessmen and shoppers during the daytime in a dark oak-panelled room. In the evenings, double doors were opened into the White Hall where four-course meals were served. The Fifty Shilling Tailors would shortly be obliged to rename their business – suits were advertised in their windows at £6 19s 6d. The Guinness neon sign and clock disappeared when Barclays Bank acquired this site for their new bank.

Lloyds Bank on Beastmarket Hill in 1927, two years after its construction. The bank was built on the site of an earlier bank established in 1836 as Moore & Robinson's Nottinghamshire Banking Company. When the 1920s building was demolished in 1965 many interesting discoveries were made in the foundations, including a circular stone wall which had been in the courtyard of the Carmelite Friary. The replacement bank building is a thirteen-storey monolith which, although set back from the street, breaches the building height limit of the Old Market Square.

The banking hall of Lloyds Bank, Beastmarket Hill, in 1925 with all the cashiers formally dressed. Banking companies then believed in presenting an appearance of stability in their buildings and in those days only men were employed as cashiers. The bank suffered from bomb damage in the Second World War, but still remained open.

The Cannon Film Centre, Chapel Bar, 1991. This was one of two cinemas – the other the Ritz, later the Odeon – built in the 1930s on the land in the area cleared of old houses. The Cannon opened as the Carlton Cinema in 1939 showing *Jamaica Inn* starring Charles Laughton and Maureen O'Hara. In 1959 the cinema was renamed the ABC, becoming a triple-screen theatre in 1974. After a period as the MGM, the cinema became the Cannon, reverting to the ABC before closing in 1999.

The Robin Hood Tavern, Market Street, 1988. The building had a varied history stretching back over a hundred years. Opened in 1875 as the Alexandra Skating Rink, it was converted a year later into the Talbot Palace of Varieties. After a short spell as the Gaiety Theatre, in 1901 the music hall became the city's first cinema, known as the King's Theatre. In 1913 the cinema was renamed the Scala and later the Classic before becoming the Robin Hood Tavern in 1986. The themed tavern failed two years later and the building was subsequently demolished.

A busy scene in front of the Exchange in 1906. The building was originally designed in 1724 by the mayor, Marmaduke Pennel, but was considerably altered in 1814. There were a number of public rooms including one referred to as the ballroom where exhibitions, lantern slide shows, concerts and waxwork exhibitions were held. In front of the Exchange is one of the city's early open-topped motor buses on the Sneinton and Carlton route. The Victorian shops in the background were all demolished within the next twenty years to be replaced by three well-designed office buildings.

The Shambles in 1919. These were the butchers' stalls situated behind the Exchange building. Although a great amenity to Nottingham people, with the unhealthy character of the stalls and the age of the Exchange, the authorities resolved to build a new council building. After the Exchange was demolished in 1926, the butchers moved to the West End Meat Market on Long Row West.

Cheapside in December 1921 with holly and Christmas tree stalls in the foreground. On the left is Smith's Shoe Booth and to the right the equally well-known Thraves Carpet and Linoleum shop. Set back in the middle is Kirke White's house where in 1785 the poet Henry Kirke White was born. After his early death in 1806 the building, which at the time was an inn known as the Coach and Horses, was renamed the Kirke White Tavern.

Cheapside towards Victoria Street in 1921. This was the site of the colourful flower market on Wednesdays. Within six years, all these old shops and inns behind the Exchange were to be reduced to rubble before the new arcade was built.

The Flying Horse Hotel, The Poultry, in 1900, before the façade was rebuilt in Tudor style. The building has a history of rebuilding and dates from the early eighteenth century as an inn. An application which was made in 1967 to demolish the hotel was refused but in 1987 the building was gutted and rebuilt as a shopping arcade – now named the F.H. Mall. For a number of years a fibreglass horse was situated above the entrance but this has now been removed.

Opposite: The Black Boy Hotel, Long Row East, 1952. This building is now only a memory, with the contents sold at auction after its closure in 1969. The paintings and furniture were dispersed, although the four lions from the roof are now in the castle grounds; the figure of Samuel Brunts is in the grounds of the Brunts School in Mansfield and the figure of the black boy from the lobby was recently bought at a market stall in Long Eaton. The murals by Denholm Davis in the Haddon Room, which had been covered beneath panelling, were unfortunately not saved.

Skinner & Rook, Long Row East, 1953. The business was established in 1844 by Mr Skinner who was joined by Mr Rook in 1860. For over a century the shop was noted for high-quality produce and service. Even small quantities of fruit, wine or flowers would be delivered promptly by van. Many older citizens of Nottingham will remember the last owner, the tall, elegantly dressed Alan Rook, invariably with a flower in his buttonhole. The store closed in 1955 when the wine business transferred to Maypole Yard and the building was subsequently pulled down.

❦ 2 ❦

THE INNER CITY

The Victoria railway station in 1951 when time appears to stand still.

The demolition of St Thomas's Church, Park Row, 1928. Built in 1873, the interior was decorated in Byzantine style and possessed a beautiful rood screen. When the nearby congregation moved away, the church closed in 1925 with its income divided between the churches of St Nicholas and St Matthew.

Watson Fothergill's Albert Hall in North Circus Street, *c.* 1900. The Good Templars of Nottingham laid the foundations of the hall in 1873, but after running out of money it became the Church of the People, before becoming a Wesleyan Chapel. In 1906 a disastrous fire almost completely destroyed the building which was under insured. A new Albert Hall was commissioned immediately, designed by the Methodist A.E. Lambert and mainly funded by Jesse Boot.

St George's Hall, Upper Parliament Street, 1900. The music hall opened in 1854 with a concert, the proceeds of which were donated to families of soldiers serving in the Crimean War. The interior of the hall was gas-lit, reflected by mirrors entirely covering the walls. One of the most important features of the hall was the bar from which drinks were dispensed throughout the entertainments. The hall survived until 1902 when Upper Parliament Street was widened before the laying of tramlines.

The Albert Hotel, Derby Road, 1968. This was built in the Victorian era by Scottish Brewers when brewery companies were extending from corner public houses to more substantial premises. The hotel was a staple of commercial travellers where stockrooms could be hired. Older local people may remember the hotel as the venue for wedding receptions, often after a ceremony at the nearby St Barnabas Cathedral. The hotel was demolished in 1970 before the Strathdon Hotel was built on the site.

Chapel Bar in 1933. This was, until 1743, the site of the old Bar Gate – the western entrance to the town. The building on the left was the home of Thomas Hawksley, the mayor of Nottingham, in the eighteenth century. On the right is the drapery shop of Pendred's, who later became well-known hairdressers. Although a busy junction with a police constable present, pedestrians are nonchalantly walking across the road. These buildings were all pulled down in 1961 and an underpass was built here.

Opposite, top: The Park Row Post Office in 1960. This was originally a house built on the site of the Poorhouse of St Peter's. The building is notable for the sixteenth-century windows which were saved from the old Houses of Parliament when it was burnt down in 1834. When the post office was demolished in 1961 before the construction of the extension to Maid Marian Way, the windows were removed to the Black Boy Club in Market Street.

Opposite, bottom: Empire House, Upper Parliament Street, 1988. One of T.C. Howitt's designs, it was built in 1933 for A.B. Gibson Ltd, the wholesale provisioners. When they moved from the centre of the city in 1961, Pearson Brothers acquired the property and extended their store from Long Row. The company suffered a loss of trade when the city's two shopping malls opened in the 1970s and was forced to close in 1988; the building being demolished the following year.

27

The County Hotel, The Quadrant, early 1950s. Situated next to the Theatre Royal, it was patronised by many of the actors and actresses at the theatre. The hotel had public rooms with names such as Robin Hood Lounge, Will Scarlett and Regency Rooms. It was still a period of commissionaires, bellboys and lift attendants with the accompanying feeling of a more gracious age. When the Royal Concert Hall was planned, the County Hotel's days were numbered and it closed in 1975.

The News House, Upper Parliament Street, 1949. The cinema began life in 1914 as the Parliament Picture Palace, becoming the British Cinema in 1931, changing to the Regal in 1933 and the News House in 1935. For its final year in 1957 it became known as the Odd Hour Cinema. After its demolition, the Nottingham Co-operative Society considered building a five-storey department store on the site but this plan was never executed.

The Gaumont Cinema, Wollaton Street, 1964. The cinema was built in 1908 as Barrasford's Royal Hippodrome on the site of Whitehall's factory which was destroyed in 1905 in a spectacular fire. In 1927, the theatre was converted into a cinema, with the occasional live show and in 1948 was renamed the Gaumont. The cinema closed in 1971 and was subsequently demolished.

The Empire Theatre in 1969, the year of its demolition. Many famous artists appeared on the stage here in its sixty-year existence. Charlie Chaplin made his debut here at the age of ten in 1899 as one of a clog-dancing troupe called the Lancashire Lads. In later years, Harry Lauder, Marie Lloyd, Harry Houdini, Gracie Fields, Laurel and Hardy and Max Miller all trod the boards here.

The entrance doors to the Empire Theatre. Older residents of Nottingham will possibly remember climbing the winding stone steps to the gallery where an attendant would crush as many people as possible onto the backless forms. While queueing for the theatre, the canopy gave shelter from the rain, and for refreshments the Empire Café was only a short distance along Forman Street.

The Guardian Office in the 1960s as the building was then known. Almost a century old, having been built in 1871/2, election results were declared from the second-floor balcony. The interior was a warren, apart from the machine room with its thunderous presses which could be seen through the windows on Forman Street. In 1998 the *Evening Post* moved its editorial offices to Castle Wharf House on the bank of the Nottingham Canal, while the printing was transferred to Derby. After the demolition of the building, the Corner House, an entertainment complex – was built here.

New Yard in 1924. This yard between Upper Parliament Street and Trinity Square was the birthplace of one of Nottingham's most famous characters. William Thompson, popularly known as Bendigo, was born at the house with three steps. He began prize-fighting at the age of twenty-one and during his career of sixteen years, he lost only one fight. His life then began a slow decline into alcoholism until in 1872, after hearing the reformer Richard Weaver preach, he was converted and the last few years of his life were devoted to evangelism. New Yard was later renamed Trinity Walk and redeveloped in the 1930s.

The ruins of the University College, Shakespeare Street, after the air raid of 8/9 May 1941. The front of the college received a direct hit destroying the lecture theatre and library. Across the street, the Register Office is a burnt-out shell with the consequent loss of many records. Neither of these buildings were lost forever as they were both rebuilt in their original style in the postwar years.

Milton Street in the late 1890s. The Plough & Harrow and Eastman's on the left were shortly to be demolished before the construction of the Victoria Station Hotel. The remainder of the row of buildings were not to be pulled down until the late 1920s and were replaced by Marsdens Café and the New Milton Café.

Milton Street in 1965 when all the buildings on the right were threatened with demolition before the building of the Victoria Shopping Centre. Among the businesses in this street were several well-known names — F. & R. Gibbs, E.S. Poyser, both jewellers, Capoccis, who had a number of snack bars in the city, Misses L. & M. James, milliners, and Kendalls, umbrella manufacturers.

Holy Trinity Church, Milton Street, 1900. The church was built in 1841, but exactly a century later its steeple was removed as being unsafe following damage in the Blitz on Nottingham. With the loss of the congregation the church became redundant and it was demolished in 1958, before the building of the Trinity Square car park.

The Victoria railway station in 1960, the last decade of its life. For many Nottingham people, the Victoria was considered the finer of the city's two railway stations and its loss is still lamented. The station was built by the Great Central and Great Northern Railway Companies and with no agreement on the name of the station – one suggested title was the Nottingham Joint Station – the Town Clerk stepped in and suggested the sensible name of the Victoria railway station. Dr Richard Beeching's recommendation in 1963 that the Great Central line should be closed had been foreseen prior to his report. From 1960, only semi-fast trains ran from Victoria to London and the station became more desolate with each passing year, finally closing in 1967.

The bridge between platforms at Victoria station in 1955, an ordinary scene made magical by the sun shining through the iron girders.

The almost deserted platforms of the Victoria station in 1960, illuminated by shafts of sunlight.

Milton Street from the roof of Birkbeck House in 1965. On the left is the Welbeck Hotel, well patronised for business lunches, meetings, wedding receptions and private parties. The buildings on that side of Milton Street were all scheduled for demolition within the next five years before the construction of the Victoria Shopping Centre.

The Mechanics Cinema, Milton Street, in 1963 showing John Wayne and Maureen O'Hara in *McLintock*. The building opened in 1869 as the Mechanics Hall after a disastrous fire had destroyed an earlier building. For almost half a century it was the premier meeting hall of Nottingham with many notable personalities such as Dickens, Shackleton, Scott and Conan Doyle appearing here. In 1916 the hall was converted into a cinema, but was demolished in 1964 to be replaced by Birkbeck House, incorporating shops, offices and the Mechanics Institute.

The Trinity Square car park in 1965, the year of its opening. One of the city's least attractive buildings, it has now been replaced by a monolithic shopping complex including a small, inappropriate sitting area.

Lower Parliament Street in the 1880s. In the centre is Bass & Wilford's proprietary chemist shop advertising cures for gout and corns as well as gardener's soap for insects and roses. This was the house to which William Howitt, the Quaker and writer, brought his wife Mary in 1823 and where they entertained William Wordsworth. On the left is the Original Dog and Partridge, so named to distinguish it from the Old Dog and Partridge on the opposite side of Parliament Street. These premises were pulled down in 1896 to be replaced by an enlarged Dog and Partridge, itself demolished in 1970 before the Victoria Shopping Centre was built.

The Tradesmen's Mart, Lower Parliament Street, 1890s. These were business premises on the lower floors with dwellings above, and among the traders was an engraver, clockmaker, umbrella maker, tinman and picture restorer. One of the billboards pasted on the building is advertising a performance of Haydn's *Creation* by the Nottingham Sacred Harmonic Society, as it was then known. This building was pulled down in 1897 to be replaced by Lombard House which for sixty years was occupied by R. Cripps & Company as a motor car showroom.

St Stephen's Arch in 1936. The archway led, until 1898, to St Stephen's Church and School which were pulled down stone by stone before the building of the Victoria railway station and re-erected in Bobbers Mill Road. This building then became the premises of Taylor's, the city's leading veterinary practice, with a carved stone horse above the arch. In 1935 the business moved to Canning Circus, this building remaining until 1968 when the horse was removed, to reappear in 2001 in the window of an auctioneers, Neales, before it was sold at a public auction.

The Old Corner Pin, at the junction of Clumber Street and Upper Parliament Street in 1991, shortly after its closure. Not a lost building as such, but now completely altered in character from the original eighteenth-century inn. Once named the Horse and Groom, this was the site of a maypole and one of the entrances to the town. After the building was gutted, a Disney store opened here and this has now become a Miss Selfridge store.

The Milton's Head Hotel at the corner of Milton Street and Lower Parliament Street, 1969. A Victorian pub built on the site of an eighteenth-century inn, it had the appearance of permanency but this was deceiving as it fell to the wrecker's ball in the same year, before the construction of the Victoria Shopping Centre.

Cave Chambers (also known as Garibaldi Yard), Bridlesmith Gate, 1921, The site of the Garibaldi Inn —
this could be a scene from the sixteenth century. In common with most city centre buildings, these had
underground caves which were reputed to be haunted. In 1933, when the City Council decided they were
beyond repair, the buildings were pulled down.

A row of old buildings including one Tudor structure in Bridlesmith Gate, 1921. The varied businesses include an antique shop, a cured meat shop established in 1760, a hatter and a café. In 1945 these buildings were inexplicably pulled down, robbing the city of a priceless link with the past.

Bottle Lane in 1975; a street as old as Bridlesmith Gate although these buildings are mainly Victorian, apart from the Queen Elizabeth public house which was rebuilt in 1928 in Tudor style. George Wick was then a familiar and friendly figure in the doorway of his flower shop at the bottom of Bottle Lane. That building, now Waterstone's, remains – but the buildings further up the lane have since been demolished.

The House of Correction, Glasshouse Street, 1890. The prison was built in 1860/1 on the site of an earlier gaol and initially contained 120 cells for male prisoners. The Governor's House built in Gothic style is to the left of the main gateway, with the Porter's Lodge to the right. In 1891 the prisoners were transferred to a new prison at Bagthorpe – this building remaining until 1900.

The Central Market, King Edward Street, 1970. Although busiest on Wednesdays and Saturdays it was a daily market with country folk bringing produce to sell on a regular basis. In a separate area of the market were the fish stalls where one could indulge in a dish of cockles, whelks or, alternatively, mushy peas. The market closed in 1972 when the stallholders moved their businesses to the new Victoria Shopping Centre.

❦ 3 ❦

AROUND THE CASTLE

Sheriff John Reckless's house at the corner of Spaniel Row and Friar Lane in 1922. In 1649 John Reckless was converted by George Fox, the founder of the Society of Quakers. George was given shelter here after his imprisonment for disturbing a service at St Mary's Church. The unusual car parked outside the house is a Trojan, a long-forgotten make. All these properties were to be demolished later in the 1920s when Friar Lane was widened.

The Gate Hangs Well, Brewhouse Yard, 1906. A board outside read 'This gate hangs well, and hinders none, refresh and pay and travel on', but following the closure of the inn in that year, the sign was removed. Perhaps not as old as the Trip to Jerusalem, but looking very ancient, this inn was one of several in Brewhouse Yard, beyond the limits of the town. Also known as the Hanging Gate, the tavern was demolished in 1909.

The Trip to Jerusalem, Brewhouse Yard, 1906. The most famous inn in Nottingham, not a lost building but the exterior now much changed. The sign claiming the inn to be the oldest in England is not yet in evidence.

St Nicholas' Church School and Institute, Castle Road, 1952. The school opened in 1859 when the district was densely populated, but closed in 1906, with the institute remaining until 1956 when the building was pulled down. The Peoples' College of Further Education which replaced the school is a typical 1950s building with little character and is now scheduled for demolition.

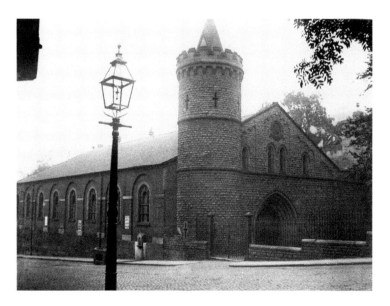

The Riding School, Castle Road, in 1924, two years before its destruction. The school was built in 1798 for the Yeomanry Cavalry when Nottingham was a garrison town, and enlarged for the Robin Hood Rifles. During the nineteenth century the building was also used by strolling players and musicians. After the military left Nottingham, the Riding School was employed for a variety of uses including a store for food during the First World War and as a sorting office for Christmas mail.

Jessamine Cottages on Gillyflower Hill or July Flower Hill, below the Castle Walls in 1923. Originally the workhouse for the parish of St Nicholas, it was built at a cost of £280 in 1724 and converted into cottages in 1815. The facilities were primitive with no running water or electricity. When the cottages were threatened with demolition in 1956 the Thoroton Society urged the City Council to improve their amenities but to no avail and this attractive feature was lost.

Castle Road in 1949. Previously known as the Hollows, it was shortly to be redeveloped losing its old-world charm. The Watson Fothergill building on the left was saved but Walnut Tree Lane, an old winding street, and Castle Terrace with its early Victorian houses, were demolished.

Old houses in Hounds Gate, viewed from St Nicholas Street in 1913. This area near the Old Salutation Inn, just visible on the left, has the appearance of being unchanged for centuries, but within twenty years these picturesque buildings were to disappear. Only the Salutation was to remain, although now substantially restored. With foresight the Hounds Gate and Castle Gate area with its medieval, Tudor and Georgian buildings could have been a great tourist attraction.

An array of chimneys viewed from the walls of the castle in the 1950s. All these houses were to be indiscriminately pulled down when the authorities began clearing the area before the building of the Peoples' College of Further Education. The prospect now from this viewpoint is unfortunately of high-rise office blocks and flats.

Hounds Gate at the junction of St Nicholas Street in 1922. On the immediate right is the Old Salutation Inn, with the appearance of a genuine old tavern. The earliest reference to the Salutation was in 1725 but the building dates from much earlier. Below the inn are three levels of caves which were in all probability intended for habitation.

Castle Gate in 1956 when the buildings in the foreground were threatened with demolition. The house on the left is seventeenth-century in the Dutch style and considered beyond restoration. It was replaced by an office block completely out of character with the adjoining Newdigate House. Set back on the right is St Nicholas Rectory, built by Watson Fothergill and yet another victim of the contractor's wrecking ball.

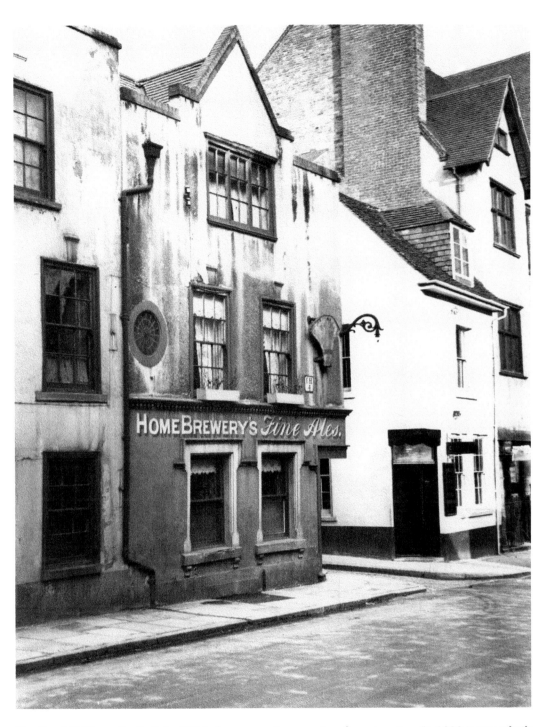

The Royal Children, Castle Gate, 1924, then a genuine seventeenth-century inn. In 1933 it was rebuilt in mock-Tudor style. The name of the inn is derived from the fable that the children of Princess Anne, daughter of James II, played with the landlord's children when she stayed in Nottingham in 1688. As the princess then had no living children, this story is only a charming legend.

One of the old properties in Spaniel Row in 1928. This was once the house of James Huthwaite, three times mayor of Nottingham in the eighteenth century. In its last days before demolition, the ground floor of the house was used as the hairdressing saloon of Henry Kirk, who was advertising hair-cutting, shaving, shampooing and singeing. After the building was pulled down he transferred his business to a new property in Friar Lane.

Spaniel Row in 1921. The building in the foreground was built in 1737 as the Church of the Society of Friends. In 1847 it became the Catholic Apostolic Church and in 1867, Copestake, Moore and Crampton, lace manufacturers, bought the building for use by their employees as a chapel. In the background is the Friar Lane Adult School. All these buildings have now gone.

Collin's Almshouses, Friar Lane, 1950. The garden was an oasis in the centre of the city for the residents of the twenty-four almshouses. These were built in 1709 under the endowment of Abel Collin, a wealthy mercer, whose father was the gunner of Nottingham Castle. The residents were allowed two shillings a week for expenses and one and a half tons of coal annually. When these almshouses, which were described as being among the finest in the country, were threatened with demolition before the construction of Maid Marian Way, there was a public outcry. The Works and Ways Committee then proposed a part-exchange of land with the Trustees of the Charity, giving the almshouses land in Hounds Gate, in exchange for part of their property, but leaving the main building untouched. Unfortunately, this plan was not adopted and the almshouses were knocked down in 1956.

Mrs Darby on the right – a resident of the Collin's Almshouses, having a chat with a neighbour in 1926. This was the finest Queen Anne building remaining in Nottingham.

The sundial above the entrance to the Collin's Almshouses, with an apt quotation from the Bible underneath. When the almshouses closed, the residents moved to a new property on Derby Road.

The Postern Gate to the Children's Hospital, Postern Street, 1922. This was built as the Free Hospital for Sick Children by T.C. Hine in 1869. The central part of the gate was brought from All Saints' Church, Annesley, and when removed from here in 1940 was taken to the Castle Museum.

The bridge over Postern Street between the General Hospital and the old Fever Wards in 1992. This was the second bridge over the street, as the first, donated in 1880 by Sir Charles Seely (a copy of the Bridge of Sighs in Venice) was so disliked by the benefactor that it was demolished and replaced by this plain brick and iron structure. The figures of saints were retained, one of which was believed to be St Luke. This bridge was pulled down in 1994, with the ironwork and figures being sold to an architectural scrap dealer.

❧ 4 ❧

THE LACE MARKET

Horne's Castle, Bellar Gate, 1928. This was a public house which was notorious for being the home in 1759 of William Horne who was convicted of the murder of a child thirty-five years earlier. He was due to be hanged on his birthday and was aggrieved to miss his plum pudding which was an unvarying part of his celebration. After his death the house was named Old Horne's Hall, before becoming a public house which was demolished in the 1950s.

Severns, Middle Pavement, 1964. Only the older citizens of Nottingham will remember dining in this fifteenth-century building. Until 1900 it was a private house and was then purchased by Severns who owned the adjoining Georgian house which had the reputation of being the finest Gentlemans' Grill Room in Nottingham. In 1939 plans were made to develop the older house as a restaurant and it was stripped of the false walls and ceilings to reveal a unique five hundred-year-old, two-storey, timber-framed building.

The doorway of Severns Georgian building on Middle Pavement. The wine-importing business was founded in 1736 by the brothers John and James Severn and was to remain a family concern for over two hundred years. The building was demolished before the construction of the Broad Marsh Centre.

Severns Yard, Middle Pavement, 1928. This, in the past, led to the stabling yard of Severns. The medieval building on the left was originally the front part of a much larger house. When plans were drawn up for the building of the Broad Marsh Centre, these buildings were condemned to be demolished, but after a concerted campaign by conservationists, the fifteenth-century building was saved and re-erected on Castle Road.

The Postern Gate Inn, Middle Pavement, 1895. This inn was built in about 1600 at the top of Drury Hill – the southern gateway to the town – the landlord's task being to close the gate each evening. A sign in the window advertises Louis Tussaud's waxworks exhibition to be held in the Albert Hall. The inn was pulled down in 1911 before the building of Postern Chambers.

Postern Chambers in 1914 – the sober replacement for the Tudor Postern Gate Inn. The building had multiple occupation, including a post office, and was to be succeeded in 1973 by a structure of no character.

The old Town Hall, Weekday Cross, 1893. This was originally built in 1744 replacing the medieval timber-framed Guildhall, and rebuilt in 1791. When the Town Hall was demolished in 1895 before the building of the Great Central Railway, the clock survived and after being presented to Sir John Turney, it was later installed on the corner of Perry's Boulevard Works on Radford Boulevard where, with a new face, it still remains.

Drury Hill with an errand boy trudging up the slope, 1946. Besides being historically important as the road from the south in the Middle Ages, it also had a number of interesting shops including antique, book and leather goods businesses, the latter giving off a pungent odour, a reminder of the days when Narrow Marsh was the centre of the tanning trade. Higham's shoe shop near the top of the hill was established here in 1848 and when Drury Hill was bulldozed they moved onto Bridlesmith Gate.

Weekday Cross, 1930. Originally the centre of the English Borough, it possessed a market until 1800. The Barley Mow public house was sufficiently close to the Shire Hall to enable lawyers and witnesses to hurry out of the courts between appearances for refreshments. A replica cross for the Thomas Sandby original was positioned here in 1993.

High Pavement, 1931. The house with a plaque on the wall was a boarding school run by the mother of Henry Kirke White, the poet. He lived here from 1798 to 1806. Among his works is a volume of poems entitled *Clifton Grove*, published in 1803. He burnt himself out through overwork and died in St John's College, Cambridge, in 1806. This building was one of the casualties of the Blitz and was subsequently demolished.

The Old High School, Stoney Street, 1922. The school was founded in 1513 by Dame Agnes Mellers in memory of her husband, Richard Mellers, a bellfounder. She provided for an annual service at St Mary's Church on the anniversary of her husband's death, followed by the distribution of bread, cheese and ale 'to the mayor, aldermen and certain others.' The school moved to Arboretum Street in 1868 and after being used by the Women's Voluntary Service during the Second World War, this building was pulled down in 1970.

An historic shop in Goose Gate, 1934. It was in 1866 that Mary Boot and her son Jesse, then aged sixteen, opened a herbalist shop here at No. 38, having moved from No. 6 Goose Gate where John Boot, Jesse's father, had begun trading in 1849. Jesse was a natural-born businessman, buying goods in bulk and selling at reduced prices. His move to new premises at 16–20 Goose Gate in 1881 was the beginning of his expansion to other sites in Nottingham and beyond. The photograph of Marriott's shortly before the demolition of the premises was used by Boots for a famous reconstructed image of Jesse's first shop.

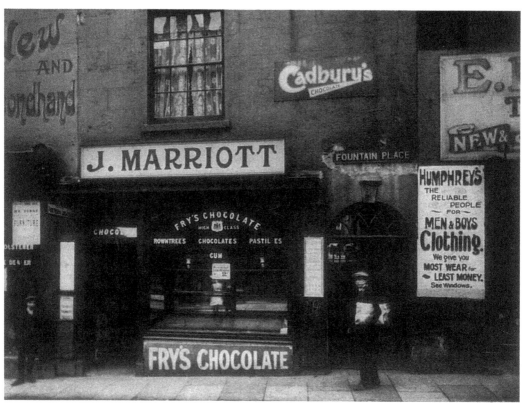

The Old Theatre Royal, St Mary's Gate, 1928.
Built in 1760 by James Whitley, his theatre
company staged 'seasons' to coincide with the
town's August racing festival and Goose Fair.
Edmund Kean, Sarah Siddons and Paganini all
performed here. In 1865 when the Theatre Royal
opened in Theatre Square, this theatre became
the Royal Alhambra Music Hall and in 1883 was
opened as a restaurant before being converted
into a warehouse in 1901. During the Blitz the
building suffered a direct hit.

The Windmill Inn, Fletcher Gate, 1910.
A seventeenth-century inn, originally known as
the Four Coffins, it had survived for over three
centuries when it became a victim to a road-
widening scheme which had little justification.

Long Stairs in 1922, when it was still one of the routes from High Pavement to Narrow Marsh, with a lone fig tree desperately clinging to the rock face. The stairs were closed in 1933 when the last old houses were cleared from Narrow Marsh but the remaining top steps can still be seen from Commerce Square. In the distance is St Patrick's Church which was to remain until 1979.

Short Stairs, 1922. The prominent Tudor building became a school in the eighteenth century and was later owned by Mrs Kate Burrows, a lace finisher, one of the many in the district. Most of these buildings have now disappeared but the stairs, one of the last old footpaths to the Marshes, have been restored.

The Town Arms, Plumptre Square, 1972. This was originally the Rugged Staff. Situated at the foot of Malin Hill, it was honeycombed with caves which were revealed when the pub was eventually pulled down after a disastrous fire in 1987.

The Old Cricket Players Inn, Barker Gate, 1997. As the sign proclaims, the pub was rebuilt in 1884 near a Sneinton cricket field. When the Ice Stadium was built nearby, the Cricket Players was a favourite of both fans and teams. The pub was pulled down in 2003 and an apartment block named the Ice House was built here.

❧ 5 ❧

BROAD MARSH

Broad Marsh viewed from the castle grounds in 1953. Although most of the slum properties of Broad Marsh were demolished in the 1920s and '30s, there was still an area of poor housing at the foot of Walnut Tree Lane to be cleared and this was achieved by the end of the 1950s.

The Collin Almshouses, Carrington Street, 1930. The almshouses were built by the Trustees of the Collin Charity in open fields between 1831 and 1834. By the time of this photograph, they were becoming increasingly dilapidated and the decision was taken to sell them and to build new almshouses on Derby Road. The Co-operative Wholesale Society paid £60,000 for them in 1936, intending to build showrooms and offices on the site, but the outbreak of war prevented this. In 1954, the City Council bought and demolished the property and used the land as a temporary car park.

The junction of Carrington Street and Broad Marsh, known as Lucky Corner, 1964. Second only to the lions in front of the Council House, this was a favourite meeting place for friends. On the right is Burton's the Tailors in a 1920s building, offering made-to-measure suits at a price within the reach of most workmen. When the building was demolished before the construction of the Broad Marsh Shopping Centre, the nine carved heads of notable Britons on the façade were removed and attached to a pillar at the foot of Garners Hill.

A horse-drawn bus at the Walter Fountain in 1948, brought out of retirement to celebrate the Golden Jubilee of the Nottingham Corporation Transport Department. The service began in September 1947 and ran from Broad Marsh along Castle Boulevard for a fare of one shilling. The fountain was built in 1866 in memory of John Walter MP, the chief proprietor of *The Times*, by his son, also John Walter. Road improvements led to the fountain being dismantled in 1950.

Sussex Street at the corner with Harrington Street in 1928. This street, once known as Turn Calf Alley was one of the main streets of Broad Marsh. While appearing picturesque, the houses were becoming more and more squalid, and the City Council began the clearance of the area, rehousing the inhabitants on new estates in the outer suburbs.

Shops on Sussex Street in 1928 showing their age. The date-stone on this building is 1656 with the letters LWF. This indicated that the property was then owned by William and Phoebe Lealand. William Lealand was a dyer and in 1655 he bought 5 acres of land which had been part of the estate of the Franciscan or Grey Friars.

Red Lion Street, otherwise known as Narrow Marsh, in 1933, when these houses were already condemned. Only one property was spared – the white building on the far right – the Loggerheads public house.

John Player's original factory in Broad Marsh in 1968, the year of its demolition. John Player commenced his business in 1862 selling manure and loose tobacco on Beastmarket Hill and expanded into rolled cigarettes. He became one of Nottingham's major entrepreneurs, founding a company which by 1939 was employing over 7,500 workers.

Wasteland in Broad Marsh in 1933, cleared of most of the area's buildings. In the centre right is one of the infamous blocks of back-to-back houses, in which were packed dozens of families without adequate facilities. Some of the dispossessed moved into Cliff Road, but the majority were rehoused in new estates in west Nottingham.

The Broad Marsh bus station in 1965. After the clearance which took place in the 1930s this land remained unused until after the Second World War when funfairs, exhibitions and other occasional events were held here. In 1953 a bus station and car park was sited on this land and, although only intended to be temporary, it was to remain until 1970.

St John the Baptist Church, Leenside, after the Blitz which devastated it. Designed by Sir George Gilbert Scott in 1844, this church was one of the worst casualties of the city during the war. With its congregation having already moved away, the church was never rebuilt.

Broad Marsh towards Lister Gate, 1931.
The Black's Head was shortly to close and
be replaced by the Tower public house.
In the eighteenth century the house was
occupied by Cassandra and Elizabeth
Willoughby, relations of Lord Willoughby
of Wollaton Hall, and afterwards by
Captain George Cartwright – the last man
in Nottingham to indulge in the sport of
hawking. The Tudor building of Severn &
Co. remained until 1968 when the Broad
Marsh Centre development began.

The railway arches under the Great Central
Railway line in Broad Marsh, 1967. This
was the year of the last passenger train on
the line, although goods trains continued
to use it for a further year. The arches,
with access from Malt Mill Lane, continued
to be used by small businesses until the
construction of the Nottingham Express
Transit line in 2001.

Trent Street in 1929. Two splendid motor cars, a Wolseley and a Ford, are outside A.R. Atkey's motor spares warehouse. On the right is one of Boots offices, originally Atkey's main premises. The viaduct on the left carried the Great Central Railway line and is now the site of the tram terminus. On the skyline is the High Pavement Unitarian Chapel which was opened in 1876 and contains wonderful stained-glass windows designed by Edward Burne-Jones. Following its closure as a chapel in 1980, the building was converted in 1988 into a lace museum and has now become the Pitcher and Piano, a bar and restaurant.

The Boots head office on Station Street in the 1920s. The building was originally Hine & Mundella's hosiery factory, built in 1851, but in 1898 Jesse Boot began leasing rooms in the block and in 1912 he completed the purchase of the whole factory for £22,000. From his first-floor office at the corner of the building, Jesse managed a company with over 500 branches, becoming a retail empire without rival. After Boots moved their head office to Beeston in 1968, the land remained undeveloped until in 2002 Capital One built Loxley House on the site.

St Patrick's Roman Catholic Church in Plumptre Square, 1971. The church with an adjoining school was built in 1880 for the expanding population of the area. In 1960, St Patrick's closed and a new church was built in the Meadows, the old church being demolished in 1979.

St Philip's Church, Pennyfoot Street, 1960. The church was built in memory of Thomas Adams, the lace manufacturer. As with the nearby St Patrick's, the loss of its congregation forced the closure of the church in 1961. The site was then used for the building of a research block for Boots.

The London Road High-Level railway station in 1935, with, in the background, Boots warehouses. The station was built in 1897 by the Great Northern Railway Company, which was later absorbed by the London North Eastern Railway Company. It was mainly used for excursion traffic – half-day trips to Leeds for 4s 6d are advertised. The line was closed for passenger traffic in 1967 and the station booking office became the Great Central and later Hooters – both bar/restaurants – before being demolished. The Boots warehouses were built in 1914 and were to remain until 1996, with the land still only partially developed.

A troop of cavalry leaving the Low-Level railway station in 1952. These soldiers from the Royal Army Service Corps are on their way to Wollaton Park to give a mounted display in the Bath & West Show. They are wearing black armbands in mourning for the late King George VI. In the background is the East Croft gasworks with two gasholders – this a time when the city possessed three gasworks. After the East Croft works were demolished Boots built a new warehouse on the land.

ᕯ 6 ᕯ

THE MEADOWS TO THE
RIVER TRENT

The Meadows from Nottingham Castle, 1972. It is now difficult to imagine this area when it was a meadow stretching to the River Trent, which each springtime was carpeted with purple crocuses. The second half of the nineteenth century saw the development of this land with the whole district filled with hundreds of terraced houses, schools and factories. A century later, most of the houses were razed to the ground to be replaced by featureless terraces and precincts.

The Canal Tavern, Canal Street, shortly before its closure in 1996. Like the nearby Narrow Boat, this public house is a reminder of the days when the Nottingham Canal was a busy commercial waterway. After the building's demolition, the *Nottingham Evening Post* built new editorial offices on the land.

The James Store building, Carrington Street, 1950. Built in the early twentieth century by Charles James, the department store was initially successful but during the 1930s the business declined and closed in 1939. During the war the Ministry of Pensions occupied the building which later became the showrooms of the East Midlands Electricity Board, closing in 1968 before the construction of the Broad Marsh Centre.

Bridgeway Hall, Arkwright Street, 1965
– a year after its closure. A notice on the
board outside reads 'Opened in 1864, now
a hundred years not out'. The hall began
as the Arkwright Wesleyan Chapel and in
1925 became the Methodist Home Mission.
Penny pictures were shown on Tuesdays
and when sound was added to cinema films
these were advertised as the 'Tuppenny
Talkies'. After the chapel was pulled down,
a new Bridgeway Hall was built on the site.

The Poet's Corner, Kirke White Street East,
1972. The pub's name is an allusion to
Henry Kirke White, the Nottingham poet
most famous for his first volume of verse
entitled *Clifton Grove*, reflecting his love of
the countryside close to the River Trent.
Since the demolition of this building in
1975 a public house of the same name has
been built in the nearby Bridgeway Centre.

A row of distinctive buildings in Arkwright Street in 1973. Baldwin House, the mock-Tudor building on the left, was the head office of H.J. Baldwin & Company, who were cable-cover manufacturers. The houses beyond were among the most prepossessing buildings on Arkwright Street but they were all marked for demolition in the general clearance of the Meadows.

The old Imperial Cinema, Wilford Road, 1975 – the year before its demolition. The cinema opened in 1916 as the Imperial Picture Palace when cinemas were built to impress their patrons. This was one of the earliest victims of the television age, closing in 1957 when it became the offices and showrooms of a builders' merchant.

The Cremorne Hotel, Queen's Drive, 1972. Rebuilt in 1917, the public house was popular with folk heading for the Victoria Embankment or Wilford. The land adjoining the pub was the site of the Cremorne Wakes, adding to the attraction of this riverside venue. The Cremorne has now been demolished, having been replaced by a housing development.

The General Gordon, London Road, 1987, one of the many public houses named after the hero of Khartoum. After a century as the Gordon, in 1992 the pub was unaccountably renamed Old Tracks. The new name was short-lived, the pub closing in 1995 to be converted into flats for the charity Family First. A new road layout in 2000 brought about the demolition of the building.

The Midlands Industrial Exhibition at Trent Bridge, 1903. The Industrial Pavilion was only a small part of the exhibition – the majority was a huge funfair. Besides a rollercoaster, there was a water chute, a maze, a Biograph pavilion, a concert hall, a Japanese tea-house and an Electric Theatre. The exhibition was only intended to be temporary, but a fire which broke out in July 1904 in one of the prefabricated buildings quickly spread around the site, forcing its early closure.

The Globe Cinema, Trent Bridge, 1955. Built in 1912 with unusual architectural features, the cinema survived until 1961, when it was converted for a year into a bingo hall. The Globe and most cinemas of the period then showed films continuously – cinema-goers would often see the end of a film before the beginning – the origin of the phrase 'This is where we came in.'

The Burton Homes, London Road, 1971. These were established in 1859 by Ann Burton for twenty-four widows, widowers or unmarried persons of good character and in needy circumstances. They were all allowed 15s a month and an annual supply of coal. When the homes were closed in 1973 the residents moved to a new complex in the Meadows.

The Plaisaunce Yacht Club, Wilford Lane, 1951. This was built in 1897 by Jesse Boot as a summer house where he could entertain friends and staff of his company. The continental style chalet was large enough for his family and also had a dance hall and tea rooms for guests. The grounds were laid out for sporting events which took place throughout the summer. Florence Boot, Jesse's wife, who took great interest in her 'girls', organised tea parties and concerts for them, and arranged for their safe return home. After Jesse's virtual retirement from the management of the company in the 1920s, the Plaisaunce became the Boots Sports Club and in 1932 was opened as the Plaisaunce Yacht Club. In 1961 the building was pulled down and the Rivermead flats were built on the site.

The North Wilford power station and the Clifton Colliery on the bank of the River Trent in 1947. The power station – a City Council undertaking opened in 1925 – was conveniently situated for water and coal. The Clifton Colliery was originally owned by the Clifton family and in 1943 became the first coal mine to be nationalised to ensure coal supplies to the adjoining power station. The colliery closed in 1969, to be followed in 1981 by the power station.

The bridge over the Fairham Brook at the beginning of the walk to Clifton Grove, 1933. In the background is the Round House, which was a tea-house on the Clifton Hall estate. One of the pleasures for Nottingham people in the past was to cross the River Trent and either picnic or have tea at the Round House or at a cottage in Clifton. The bridge and folly were demolished when the construction of the Clifton Bridge commenced in 1954.

A thatch-roofed cottage in Glapton Lane, Clifton, 1952 – the year in which the village was incorporated into Nottingham. Within two years this scene had changed completely when this building and many other old structures disappeared at the time of the building of the Clifton council estate. Fortunately, the houses surrounding Clifton Green were preserved, although enclosed on three sides by modern buildings.

St John the Baptist Church, Colwick, 1925. The church was built by Sir John Musters in 1684 and contained many monuments to the Byron and Musters families. During the 1930s the church was allowed to fall into disrepair and in 1936 was closed with the monuments removed to Newstead Abbey and All Saints' Church, Annesley. Shortly afterwards the roof of the nave collapsed and Colwick Church is now only a picturesque ruin.

The Round House, Colwick, 1956. This folly, separated from Colwick Hall by the straight mile racecourse, was becoming increasingly dilapidated. In 1967 after the straight mile course ceased to be used, the Round House was demolished and the Candle Meadow housing estate, as well as a pub logically called the Starting Gate, was built on the land.

❦ 7 ❦

ST ANN'S & SNEINTON

Princess Terrace leading from Shelton Street to Northumberland Street in 1968, with the Princess Royal public house on the left already boarded up. Of the fifty pubs in the district before the clearance in the 1970s, only five remained in the new St Ann's.

The Union Road Post Office in the 1880s. William Palmer and, after his death in 1926, his daughter Dorothy, ran the post office for almost a century. He was a keen amateur photographer and she, besides being the postmistress, ran a dancing school in the room above the post office. Previously a ballerina, she is remembered for being very strict but an excellent teacher. As well as being a post office, it was also a chemist shop, which remained almost unchanged throughout the Palmers' ownership and when it closed in 1964 the drug squad were called to remove all the drugs which remained.

Opposite, top: Lammas Lodge, Millstone Lane (subsequently Huntingdon Street), 1930. The building, built in 1860, was also known as St Michael's Police Lodge, being situated on the edge of St Michael's Recreation Ground. This ornate building was a victim of the wholesale demolition of St Ann's but the bells and borough arms were saved and removed to the Brewhouse Yard Museum.

Opposite, bottom: The junction of Glasshouse Street, Charlotte Street and York Street, known as Cox's Corner, *c.* 1890. This was the centre of a highly populated district, notorious for its neglected houses. George Cox's draper's shop has the ubiquitous boys ranged in front of the store's windows. All these buildings were shortly to be razed by the railway company before the construction of the Victoria railway station, saving the Corporation the cost to itself.

The Empress Bingo, also known as the Empress Social Club, 1973. This began life in 1928 as the New Empress Cinema, replacing the Empress Cinema on King Edward Street. In 1960, the beginning of the decade which saw many suburban cinemas close, the New Empress was converted into a bingo hall. The general clearing of St Ann's claimed this hall – its neighbour the Locarno Bingo was, however, spared.

The Britannia Hotel, Beck Street, 1972. Opened in 1934 by the Home Brewery Company, it was both a public house and residential hotel. In 1964 the hotel became a Berni Inn, but in 2000 the building was demolished to be replaced by an apartment block.

The Westminster Bank, Commercial Square, 1970. The bank, designed by Watson Fothergill, was opened in 1900 as the Nottingham & Nottinghamshire Bank. Despite objections to its destruction, this typical Fothergill building succumbed, with many other noteworthy public buildings to the indiscriminate clearance of the district.

A row of houses in Berkeley Street, 1970. These houses and those in the nearby Mowbray Street were built in 1852 by William Felkin who was then mayor of Nottingham. The land had just been released for building and Felkin was one of the advocates of model housing to improve the health of the town's population. Although still in good condition, the houses were to suffer the fate of the majority of the dwellings in St Ann's and were demolished.

The Alfred the Great public house at the corner of Roden Street and Alfred Street South, 1972. A Shipstone house on a prominent corner, this pub, like all the others in St Ann's, was the focal point for the surrounding community and was greatly missed when it disappeared.

The Craven Arms, at the corner of Woodborough Road and Alfred Street Central, 1972. One of the many Victorian pubs in St Ann's, the Craven Arms was noted for its entertainment. After its closure and demolition, a Kwik Save store was opened on the site but the venture failed.

The Robin Hood Arms, Robin Hood Street, 1972 – the year of its destruction. This was one of only two public houses in Nottingham at that time named after the legendary outlaw.

The St Anns Well Inn at the junction of St Ann's Well Road and Peas Hill Road, 1972. This was the nearest pub to St Ann's Church and at a time when few people had cars, couples who married at the church invariably had their wedding reception at the St Anns Well Inn, engaging outside caterers. One of the lost pubs of St Ann's.

Robin Hood Chase in the 1950s. When St Ann's was being developed in the nineteenth century, the Corporation laid out this tree-lined walk through the built-up areas on either side. The houses lining the Chase, which ran from St Ann's Well Road to Woodborough Road, were substantial buildings with front and rear gardens. Sadly, most of the houses on the Chase have now been bulldozed.

The junction of Coalpit Lane and Beck Street, 1927. This area was known as Swine Bar and the narrow street in the centre is Cur Lane, which after the clearance in the 1930s became Lower Parliament Street. The advertisements make interesting reading: Marie Blanche was appearing at the Empire Theatre and Sunlight Soap were giving a £1,000 guarantee of purity – a small fortune in those days. The woman on the extreme right appears to be the photographer's assistant, carrying a second plate camera.

The Old Black Lion, Coalpit Lane, 1929 – the year the public house was pulled down. This was one of many licensed premises in a crowded district – there were no less than six in this street. The posters on the pub walls mainly advertise newspapers and magazines. One ponders the future for Arsenal's £30,000 wonder team – they were to win the First Division Championship four times in the next six years. The famous St Ann's Rose Show was also being advertised, promising prizes totalling £250.

Sneinton Market in 1931 with buyers and sellers endeavouring to strike a bargain. Among the unusual objects offered for sale here have been the fifteenth-century choir stalls from St Mary's Church, which were bought 'for a song' and installed in St Stephen's Church, Sneinton, and the prison door from the Old County Gaol in the Shire Hall. Most items on sale here are more mundane, with clothing and household goods predominant in this section of the market. In 1938 this area was cleared and the Wholesale Fruit and Vegetable Market was built here, with the retail market confined to an open space close to the Victoria Baths visible in the background.

Staff at the Nottingham Ice Stadium resurfacing the ice in 1950. After a skating session or ice hockey match, the ice would be skimmed before the next event. The stadium also staged boxing matches, ice galas, religious rallies, parties, and during the Quincentenary in 1949, a Pageant of Nottingham. While not the most comfortable of arenas, the old Ice Stadium was well-regarded and was the place where Jayne Torvill and Christopher Dean began their amazing careers.

Opposite, top: Boots Print Services, Lower Parliament Street, 1988. This Art Deco building was constructed in 1939 for R. Cripps & Company as a garage and car showroom but was requisitioned by the Auxiliary Fire Service at the outbreak of the Second World War. Following the war, Boots used the building as a garage prior to converting it into offices. The building was demolished in 1998 to make way for the National Ice Centre.

Opposite, bottom: The Nottingham Ice Stadium, Lower Parliament Street, 1997 – the year before it was pulled down. The stadium was built just before the Second World War and was immediately commandeered by the Air Ministry and not relinquished until 1946. The Nottingham Panthers ice hockey team was then formed with Sandy Archer as their coach and featuring many fine players such as Chick Zamick, Les Strongman and Dick Halversen in the team. In 1980 the Panthers were re-formed and now attract large crowds in the new National Ice Centre.

Wool Alley, *c.* 1900. This street of stockingers' cottages ran between Woolpack Lane and Barker Gate, one of the many alleys in the district. The entrance to the street was through a low passage and this enclosure formed a small world for the young girls in the photograph. Wool Alley was demolished, without great loss, in the slum clearances between the two world wars and the buildings which replaced it have now also disappeared. In their place is the main arena of the National Ice Centre.

Regent Hill, off Carlton Road, 1950. This small area of Sneinton Elements was scheduled to be demolished – several houses were already empty – to be replaced by council houses and renamed the Chedworth Estate.

A service held in the burnt-out shell of St Christopher's Church, Colwick Road. This was one of the casualties of the Blitz on Nottingham on the night of 8 May 1941. The church received a direct hit from a German bomb, causing the roof to collapse and smashing all the windows and pews. A few days later, after the debris had been removed, a service of rededication was held by the Revd Mr Ralph. The most extraordinary ceremony was held on 17 May 1941 when local girl Marian Smith married Fred Naylor in the gutted church, filled with the local community determined to prove that normal life could continue. This building was not entirely lost as the church was rebuilt after the war.

The White City Stadium in 1936. Olympic Speedway racing began in Trent Lane in 1929, a year after the stadium opened for greyhound racing. Crowds of up to 7,000 spectators watched the Nottingham Olympic team, but after several closures, motorcycle dirt-track racing finally ended in Nottingham in 1935. Greyhound racing continued here until 1970 when at the final meeting, 'In Memoriam' cards were distributed to the spectators. After the stands were dismantled, several industrial units were built here.

❦ 8 ❦

NORTH & WEST NOTTINGHAM

Kennel Hill, off Mansfield Road, 1932. This row of eighteenth-century cottages was originally named Chimney Hill, presumably because of the very tall chimneys on the houses. A sign on the garden wall announces the proposed leasing of the land for building purposes. On the left a Bluecoat schoolboy in his traditional uniform with a bib is emerging from the schoolyard.

St Helen's Street, 1922. The house in the middle of this street between Ilkeston Road and Derby Road was where John Leavers perfected his bobbin and carriage machine capable of producing intricate patterns in lace in 1813. Up to a decade ago, the area's biggest manufacturer, Guy Birkin Ltd, was still using gigantic Leavers machines to produce the finest lace. This street of houses was demolished in 1959, but a plaque on a nearby wall commemorates the lace machine inventor.

Old Peveril Prison, previously the Radford Workhouse in St Peter's Street, 1928. This was the last location of the Court of the Honour of Peveril which was instituted by William Peveril in 1113 as a court of pleas for the recovery of small debts. The High Stewardship of the Court was called the Honour of Peveril. Sittings were first held in the Chapel of St James, Friar Lane, but moved to the Shire Hall in 1316 and to Basford in 1368. In 1804 the court and prison were established behind the White Hart at Lenton before moving to Radford in 1842. The last three feudal courts, including the Peveril Court, were abolished in 1849. This eighteenth-century building was then converted into two houses and eventually demolished in 1968.

The last remains of Nottingham Barracks, off Derby Road, 1921. These were built by William Stretton and were first garrisoned by the 7th Light Dragoons. Innkeepers of the town welcomed the building of the barracks – previously troops had been quartered with them for little recompense. The barracks were closed in 1861 when Nottingham ceased to be a garrison town. Various events took place here in later years, but most of the buildings were demolished in 1871.

The prisoner of war camp in Wollaton Park, 1951. During the Second World War the park was requisitioned by the War Office, but it was not until 1944 that any great use was made of it. It was then that the US paratroopers of the 508th Regiment of the 82nd Airborne Division arrived and were billeted in tents here. After the war, Italian and German prisoners of war were brought here and housed in Nissen huts. Although most of the prisoners had left by 1948, it was not until 1952 that the huts were dismantled.

The Crown Hotel at the corner of Radford Marsh and Wollaton Road in 1934, shortly before its closure. The pub was scheduled for demolition in a road-widening scheme, with the licence being transferred to the new Crown Hotel built a short distance away.

The Windmill Inn, Alfreton Road, in the mid-1960s – towards the end of its life. The pub, dwarfed by the new tower blocks of flats on Hartley Road, was shortly to be replaced by a new public house on the same site. The men in the photograph seem intent on enjoying one of the pub's last days.

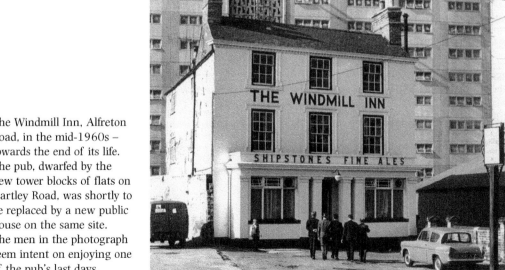

An aerial view of the Raleigh Cycle Company works, Triumph Road, 1960. Between the two world wars the company, which was already the largest manufacturer of bicycles in the world, continued to expand bringing the factory site to over 60 acres. With the increase in car ownership in the 1960s, Raleigh began to specialise in classic machines such as the RSW II, the Chopper and mountain bikes. Competition from Asian countries saw the workforce drop from a high of 7,000 in the 1950s to around 800 by the end of the century. In 2001 the company closed its Nottingham factories and moved to Eastwood where bicycles made to Raleigh design are now imported. The site of the Nottingham factories has since been used for the Jubilee Campus of the University of Nottingham.

Player's No. 2 Factory in 1972 – an uninspiring name for a distinctive building. The factory was opened in 1932 when the company's production was increasing rapidly. To work at one of the three major city employers – Players, Boots and Raleigh – was to be assured of secure employment. This building was closed in 1981 and all production was transferred to the Horizon factory in Lenton. The No. 2 Factory was demolished in 1987 with only the public clock saved and now located in the Castle Retail Park on the site of the factory.

Gauntley Street Mill in 1925, known locally as the 'Mill in the hole', one of several watermills on the banks of the River Leen. This building, with the old houses adjoining it, was reaching the end of its life – flour was no longer ground here, and the area was shortly to be redeveloped.

A general shop on Commercial Road, previously Quarry Road, Bulwell, 1925. Probably one of the smallest shops in Nottingham, James Bardsley, besides advertising as a grocer and fruiterer, also described himself as a fishfryer. The building was pulled down in the clearance of the area in the early 1930s.

Arkers Row, Old Basford, 1965 – shortly before these houses were levelled. They had few modern facilities, but the new high-rise flats to which the inhabitants were relocated proved only marginally better, having been poorly constructed. They, in turn, were demolished within fifteen years of their erection.

Broxtowe Hall, 1928. The hall was built in about 1700 by Sir Thomas Smith of the Nottingham banking family on the site of an earlier mansion. In the 1930s when the house became unoccupied, the City Council suggested that the National Trust should purchase it or alternatively it could be used as the Aspley Library. Unfortunately, no further use was found for the hall and after demolition the land was utilised for council housing.

Aspley Hall, 1925. The hall dates from about 1600 and was part of the Wollaton Hall estate. When the park was sold in 1925, Alderman G.E. Taylor bought and occupied Aspley Hall until his death in 1965. Although efforts were made to save the house, the building was demolished and the land developed for housing.

The Adelphi Cinema, Hucknall Lane, Bulwell, 1938
– the year of its opening. The 1930s was the decade
when many suburban cinemas were built in the Art
Deco or Modernist style. The first week's attractions
at the Adelphi were Grace Moore in *One Night of
Love* and Will Hay in *Oh, Mr. Porter!* The cinema
closed in 1963 and became a bingo hall and social
club, remaining until 1997 when it became another
victim of the wrecker's ball.

The Roxy Cinema, Ribblesdale Road, 1957. The
feature film was *Affair in Havana* starring John
Cassavetes. The cinema was built in 1937 when
the new housing estates of nearby Woodthorpe
and Daybrook were being developed. As with many
cinemas faced with falling attendances in the
1960s, the Roxy became a bingo hall. The building
was pulled down in 1995 and the land was used for
housing.

The Metropole Cinema, Mansfield Road, 1971.
At that time they were showing *Charro!*, starring
Elvis Presley. Another Art Deco cinema, it had
been opened in 1937 and survived until 1973.
This futuristic building then became another
bingo hall and social club and later a Kwik Save
supermarket before being demolished in 2005.

The Essoldo Cinema, Lenton Abbey, 1952.
When this photograph was taken, the main
attraction was *Lullaby of Broadway*, starring
Doris Day. The cinema opened as the Astoria
in 1936, becoming the Essoldo in 1952 and
the Classic in 1972. After closing in 1975
the building became a bingo hall and later
a skateboard park, before succumbing to
demolition in 1994.

The Derby Road Baptist Church, 1966. Built in 1850, the church survived a major fire in 1906 before closing in 1960 when the congregation moved to the newly built Thomas Helwys Baptist Church in Lenton. After the church was demolished in 1971, the site was used for a modern office block.

The Lenton General Baptist Church, 1960. This was the year of its closure and the opening of the modern Thomas Helwys Baptist Church built on an adjoining site. The old church remained for a further eight years before being pulled down.

The Lenton United Methodist Free Church, known locally as the Tin Chapel, 1970. The church was built on a solid foundation with corrugated metal sheets for the main walls – later intended to be replaced with bricks. However, constant flooding ended plans for a permanent structure. After its closure as a church in 1900, Crampton Organs occupied the building until 1920 when Clement Pianos bought the property for their business, hiring out the basement variously as a billiard hall and furniture warehouse. In 1980 Clement Pianos sold the property to Trent Upholstery who, with a council grant, improved and extended the building. In 2002 they moved to Radford and the old chapel was then demolished to be replaced by a block of flats.

The Nazareth House, Abbey Street, Lenton, 1978. The Congregation of the Poor Sisters of Nazareth opened this home in 1881 and during the following century the sisters cared for almost 4,000 adults and children. With more exacting requirements being imposed on care homes, the decision was taken to close Nazareth House and a Farewell Mass was held on 16 July 2002. After the demolition of the house, a group of town houses was built here.

ACKNOWLEDGEMENTS

I wish to thank the following for the loan of photographs:

Alliance Boots, David Amos, Alan Atkinson, Geoff Blore, Leonard Brownlow, *Derby Evening Telegraph*, Clive Hardy, Lloyds TSB, John Lock, John Middleton, Nottingham City Council Leisure and Community Services – Local Studies Library, *Nottingham Post*, William Palmer, Picture the Past's North-East Midlands Photographic Archive, Richard Shelton, Viva Imaging and Rick Wilde. The photographs of F.W. Stevenson are reproduced by kind permission of Martin Sentance.

Once again I wish to thank Dorothy Ritchie and the staff of the Local Studies Library for their invaluable help and my wife Margaret for her editorial skills.

Highfields Lido, 1947. Opened in 1924, the same year as the University Park, the lido became a very popular attraction, It closed in 1981, open-air swimming pools having lost their appeal in Britain's unpredictable climate.